የቁጥር ተረት

THE NUMBER STORY

SMALL BOOK ONE

ENGLISH - AMHARIC

Numbers Teach Children Their Number Names

written and illustrated by

MISS ANNA

Early Reader Edition of *The Number Story 1*
Bronze Medal Winner, 2016 Wishing Shelf Book Award

Library of Congress Control Number: 2018902040

Names: Miss Anna, author.
Title: Number story : numbers teach children their number names / Miss Anna.
Description: Portland, OR: Lumpy Publishing, 2018.
Identifiers: ISBN 978-1-945977-71-8| LCCN 2018902040
Summary: The pictures and rhymes present stories which introduce numbers 0-10.
Subjects: LCSH Numeration—English--Amharic--Pictorial works--Juvenile literature. | BISAC JUVENILE NONFICTION /
Languages: English--Amharic
Classification: LCC QA141.3 .M57 2018 | DDC 513—dc23

Publisher: Lumpy Publishing
Website: www.missannabooks.com
Email: missanna@missannabooks.com

Paperback: ISBN 978-1-945977-71-8
Printed in the U.S.A.   1 3 5 7 9 10 8 6 4 2

የቁጥሮቻችን ስም
መማር ትፈልጋላችሁ?

It is very easy and a lot of fun!

በጣም ቀላል እና አዝናኝ ነው!

Say-along our little jingle

አንድ ላይ እንዝፈን!

starting from Number One!

ከአንድ ቁጥር እንጀምር!

1

ONE looks like my one finger.

፩ ✰ አንድ

ጣቴን ይመስላል::

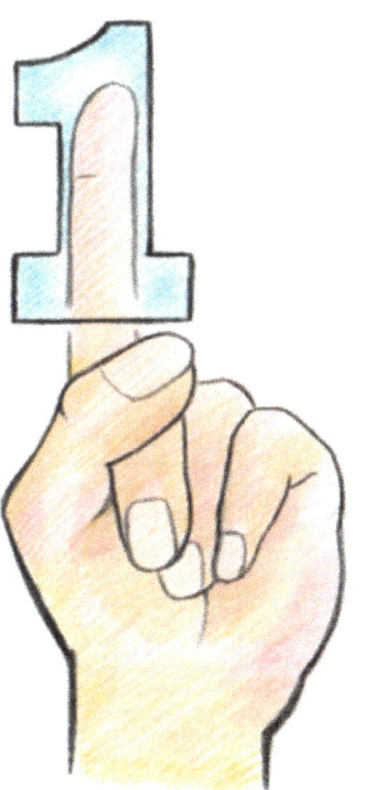
ONE!
አንድ!

2

TWO   trails a tail.

፪ ☆ ሁለት

ጭራ አለው።

A TAIL! ฤทน!

3

THREE has bumps.

፫ ሶስት

ጉብጠት አለው::

BUMPY! እይ አግብጧል!

4

FOUR carries a sail.

፬ አራት

ባለ ሸማ ጀልባ ነው።

ሸማ ይዟል።

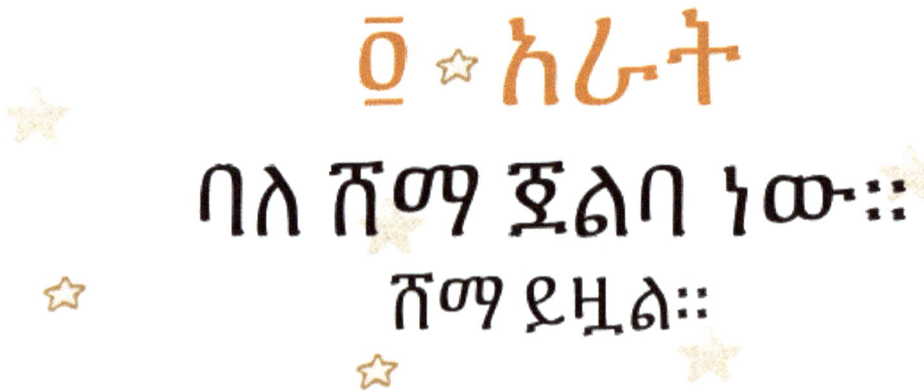

A SAIL!
የጀልባ ሸማ!

5

FIVE is a racing track.

፭ ✱ አምስት

የመኪና ውድድር መንገድ።

VROOM
CCCgo!

6

፮ ☆ ስድስት

እንደ ቀንድ አውጣ

ይታጠፋል።

A SNAIL! ቀንድ አውጣ!

7

SEVEN   has a sharp angle.

፯ ✫ ሰባት
ፋስ ነው::

OUCH!
ㅅ!

8

EIGHT is rollercoaster rails.

፰ ስምንት

ሮለርኮስተር ነው።

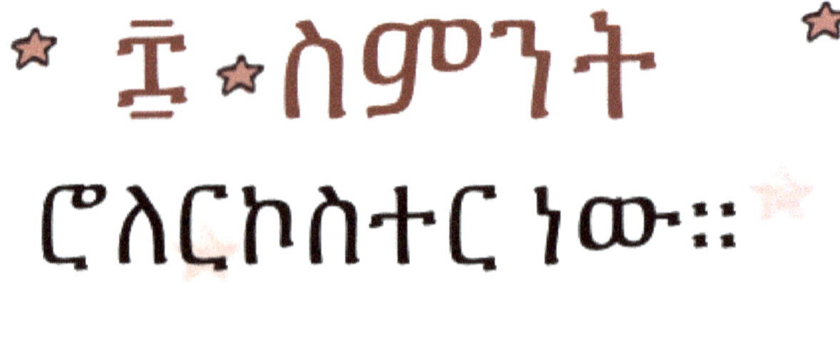

ひゃっほー！
YIPPEE!

NINE is a bubble on a stick.

፱ ዘጠኝ

የእንጪት ላይ አረፋ ነው።

A BUBBLE! አረፋ!

TEN   is an eye of a whale.

I ✫ አስር

የዓሣ ነባሪ አንድ ዓይን ነው::

ጥቅሽ!
WINK!
HELLO! እዚህ ጋ!

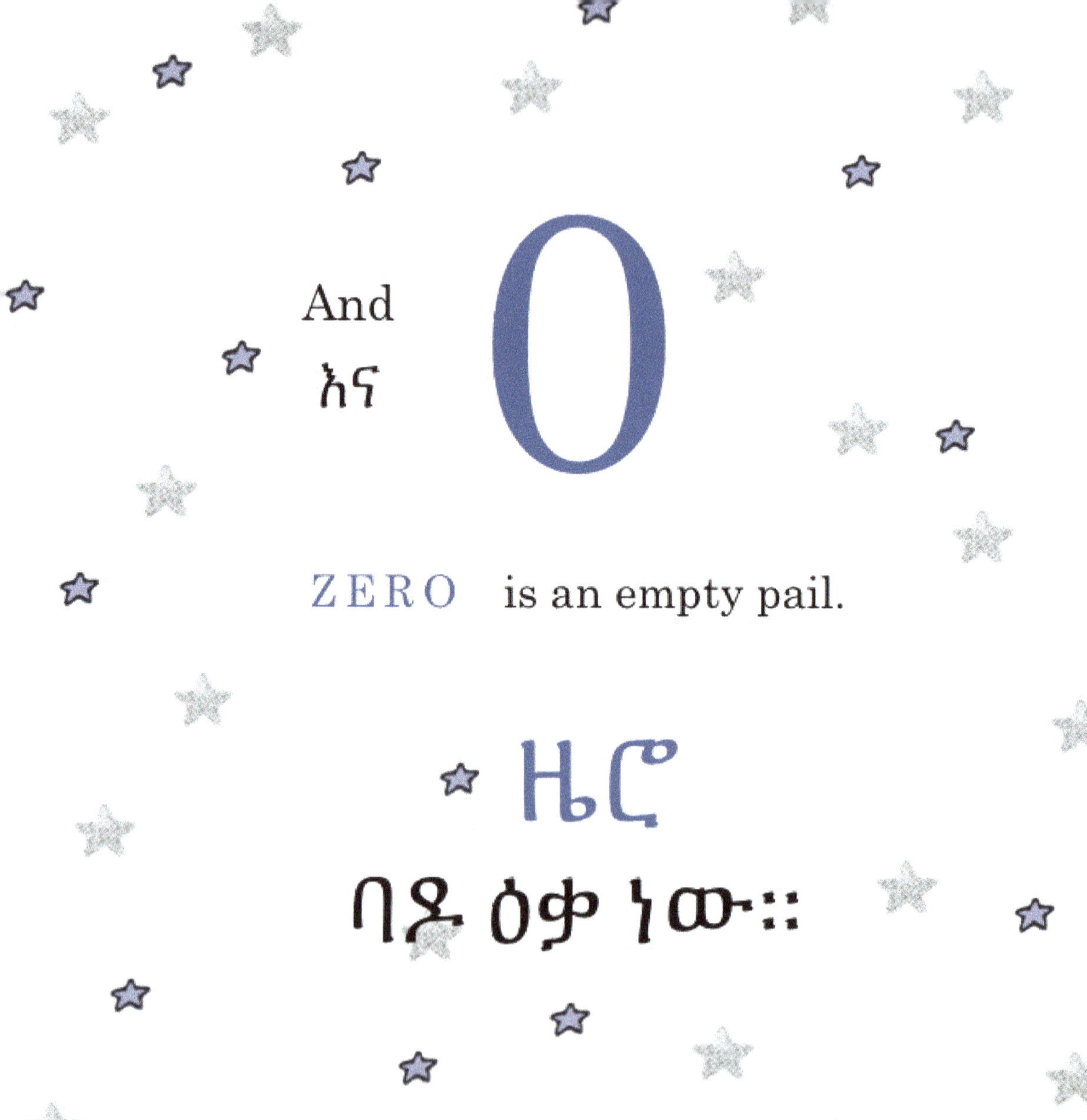
And
እና

0

ZERO   is an empty pail.

ዜሮ

ባዶ ዕቃ ነው::

IT'S
EMPTY!
ባዶ ነው!

Thank you for playing with us today.

We had a lot of fun too!

ዛሬ ከእኛ ጋር ስለተጫወታችሁ እናመሰግናለን::

ደስ የሚል ጊዜ አሳለፍን!

We are your Number friends,
Zero to Ten,
Who will be here for you~

እኛ የቁጥር ጓደኞቻችሁ ነን
ከዜሮ እስከ አስር::
ከእናንተ ጋር እዚሁ እንሆናለን::

Bye-bye now!
See you again soon!

ለአሁኑ ቻው!
እንደገና እንገናኛለን!

The Numbers are *SINGING* too!

To sing-a-long, look for Miss Anna Number Story
at your favorite music store like iTUNES.

MP3

Numbers 0-10
IDENTIFYING
& COUNTING

Numbers 11-20
& Ordinals

first, second, third...

Numbers 0-100
& Place Values

ones, tens, hundreds...

About Clocks
& Telling Time

hours, minutes, seconds

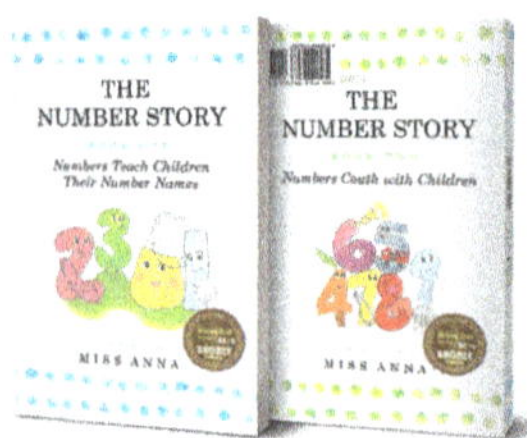

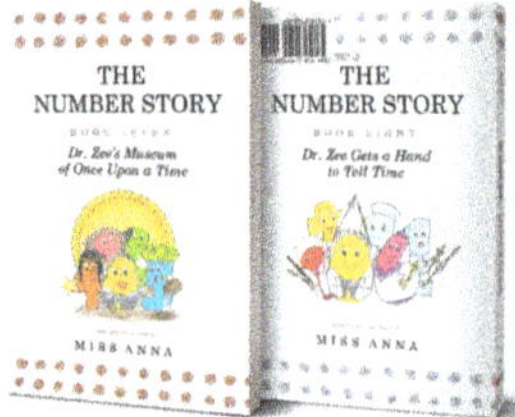

Number Story 1 & 2
isbn: 978-0-996216-48-7

Number Story 3 & 4
isbn: 978-1-945977-01-5

Number Story 5 & 6
isbn: 978-1-945977-06-0

Number Story 7 & 8
isbn: 978-1-949320-40-4

For more Miss Anna books to love,
visit us at

www.missannabooks.com

Numbers are working hard all over the world!
Come Travel the World with Us!